W9-CUO-907

ME ON THE MAP

by Joan Sweeney   illustrated by Annette Cable

Dragonfly Books™ Crown Publishers, Inc. • New York

For Peggy, John, and Tom — J. S.

To the people who put me on the map,
Mom and Dad — A. C.

DRAGONFLY BOOKS™ PUBLISHED BY CROWN PUBLISHERS, INC.

Text copyright © 1996 by Joan Sweeney
Illustrations copyright © 1996 by Annette Cable

Published by Crown Publishers, Inc., a Random House company,
201 East 50th Street, New York, NY 10022

CROWN is a trademark of Crown Publishers, Inc.

www.randomhouse.com/kids/

Library of Congress Cataloging-in-Publication Data
Sweeney, Joan.
Me on the map / by Joan Sweeney ; illustrated by Annette Cable.
p.   cm.
Summary: A child describes how her room, her house, her town, her state,
and her country become part of a map of her world.
1. Maps—Juvenile literature. [1. Maps.] I. Cable, Annette, ill. II. Title.
GA130.S885   1996   912'.014—dc20   95-14963

ISBN 0-517-70095-6 (trade)
0-517-70096-4 (lib. bdg.)
0-517-88557-3 (pbk.)

First Dragonfly Books™ edition: July 1998

Printed in Singapore
20 19 18 17 16 15 14

DRAGONFLY BOOKS IS A TRADEMARK OF ALFRED A. KNOPF, INC.

This is me.

This is me in my room.

This is a map of my room.

This is me on the map of my room.

This is my house.

This is a map of my house.
This is my room on the map of my house.

This is my street.

This is a map of my street.
This is my house on the map of my street.

This is my town.

This is a map of my town.

This is my street on the map of my town.

This is my state.

This is a map of my state.

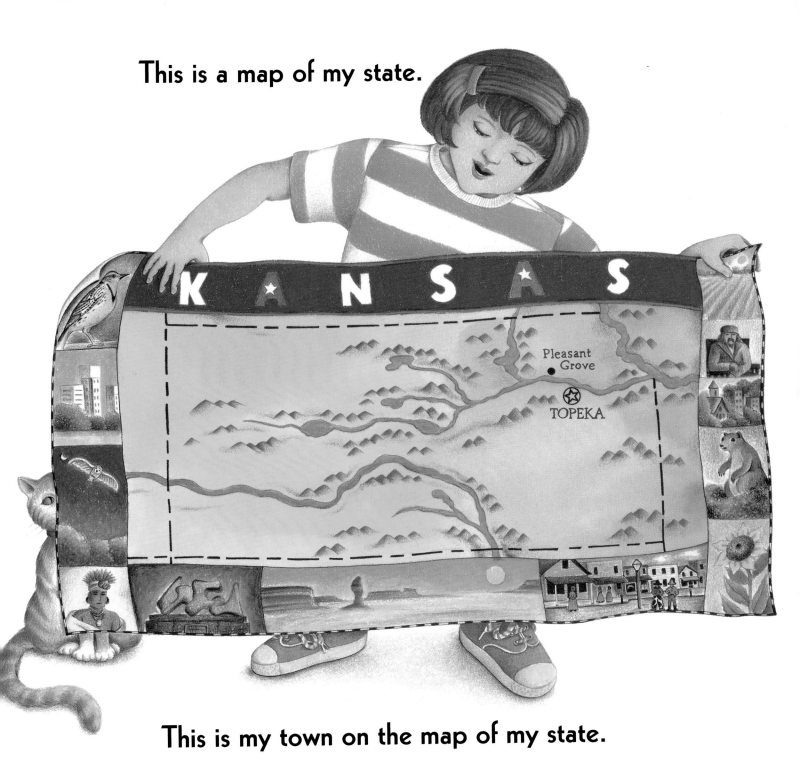

This is my town on the map of my state.

This is my country. The United States of America.

This is a map of my country.

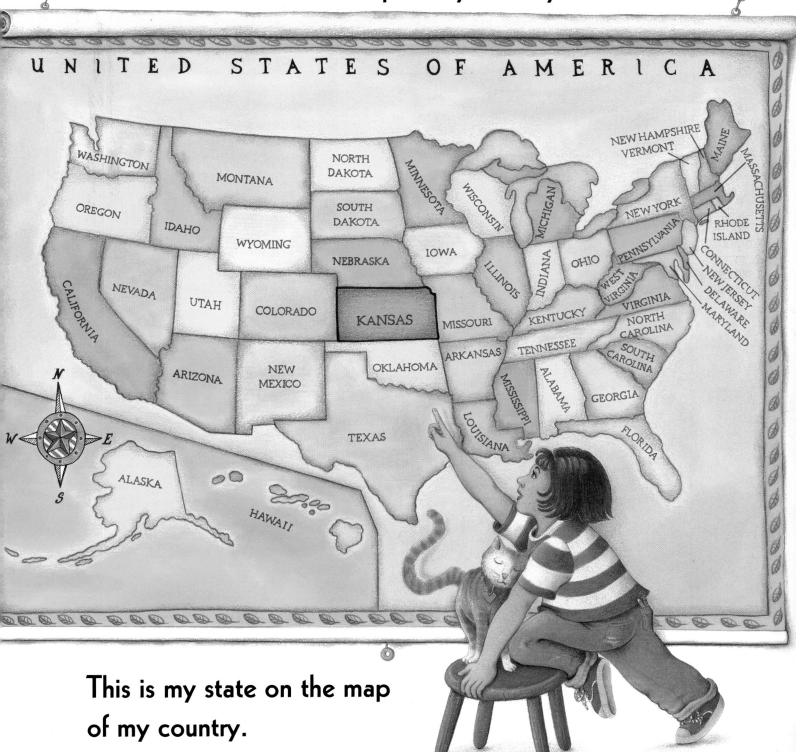

This is my state on the map
of my country.

This is my world. It is called Earth.
It looks like a giant ball.

If you could unroll the world and make it flat...

...it would look something like this map of the world.

This is my country on the map of the world.

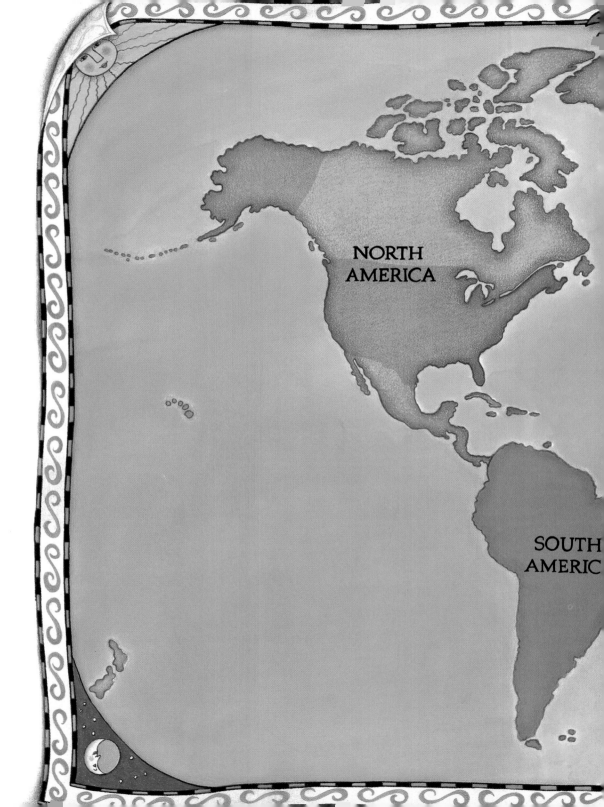

NORTH AMERICA

SOUTH AMERIC

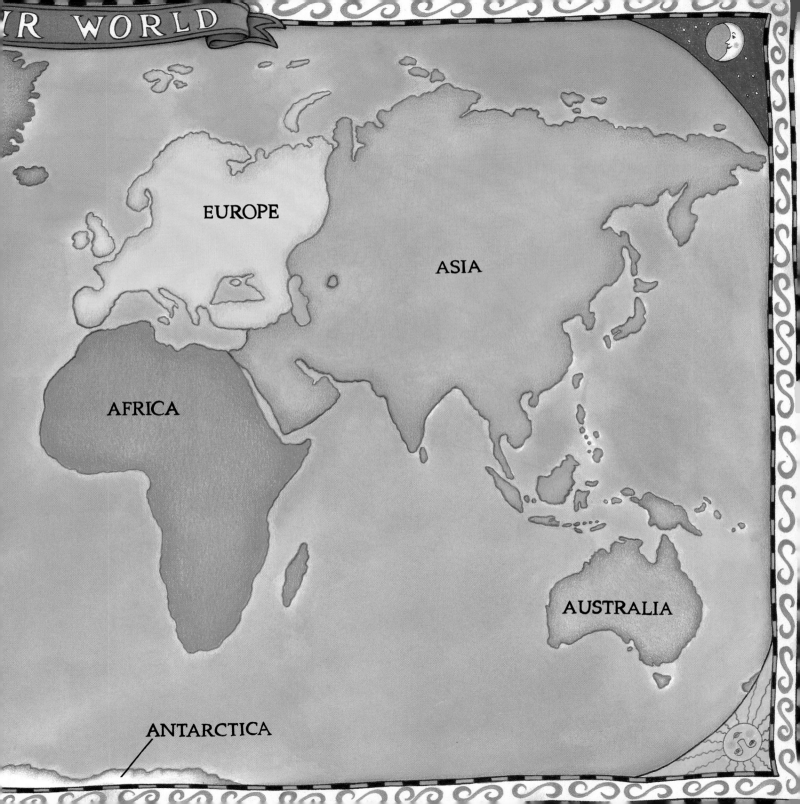

So here's how I find my special place on the map. First I look at the map of the world and find my country.

OUR WORLD

NORTH AMERICA

SOUTH AMERICA

EUROPE

ASIA

AUSTRALIA

ANT

Then I look at the map of my country and find my state.
Then I look at the map of my state and find my town.

Then I look at the map of my town and find my street.

And on my street I find my house.

And in my house
I find my room.

And in my room I find me!
Just think...

...in rooms, in houses, on streets,
in towns, in countries all over the world,
everybody has their own
special place on the map.

Just like me.

Just like me on the map.

This book belongs to:

Name_____

Street_____

Town_____

State_____

Country_____